SOLO PIANO

David Lanz
painting the Sun

T0078954

Visit David online at
www.DavidLanz.com

Painting the Sun is available on CD from Shanachie Records.
Look for it at your favorite record shop or online retailer.

Artist photograph by bhpimages.com
Original CG cover art created by David Louis Quinn

Layout and design by Carole May

ISBN 978-1-4234-6426-6

HAL•LEONARD®
CORPORATION
7777 W. BLUEMOUND RD. P.O. BOX 13819 MILWAUKEE, WI 53213

Visit Hal Leonard Online at
www.halleonard.com

David Lanz
painting the Sun

Painting the Sun – what's in a title?

The art of painting can be described as an act of individual artistic expression. The use of color, texture, shape and shading; ideas and feelings expressed visually that reflect the heart, mind and soul of the painter.

The sun is not only the center of our solar system and Earth's primary source of energy and light, but has stood throughout time as a cosmic symbol of our life force, our radiant soul (sol), and has been worshiped and revered as a god; a celestial symbol of the divine. So here, painting the sun could be said to be an expression of artistic soul …the desire to describe, and embrace the divine...the eternal.

Music wields power to captivate and transport us to a place that is unlike any other earthly or imaginary realm. The act of making music is surely one of painting with sound, added to with even more color and feeling by the experience of the listener. The soul, I believe, is expressed and engaged in these acts and inner processes, each of us in turn… painting the sun.

Listen…and see what you hear.

–David Lanz

Painting the Sun
In the opening remarks I describe in detail my artistic analysis of the title "Painting the Sun". However, the origin of this title was derived from a seemingly random and humorous experience. During early spring, on one of the daily walks I enjoy taking in my neighborhood, I strolled past the park near my home, all the while facing the warming sun. This was very pleasurable and started me to think of titles having to do with the sun. A dozen or so average ideas came to mind and then I dropped the notion. Suddenly, I was compelled to take a street I had not traveled on before. Halfway down the block I looked up at a house and noticed its Victorian gable ornament attached to the eave where the roof came to a peak. It was a sunburst pattern; the rays brightly painted in different colors. I smiled and then surprisingly blurted out loud, "painting the sun!" I had no idea in that moment what it really meant, but I loved the sound of it right away. As I continued my walk, the deeper artistic meanings flooded my mind and I laughed to myself at how the title had come about. You just never know when or where the muse will strike!

Spanish Blue

This was the last piece composed for this recording and it brought to mind the wonderful countless memories I have of touring Spain. To my ear, the improvisational nature of the right hand phrasing is faintly reminiscent of Spanish classical guitar flourishes. And the overall sweet melancholy of this piece for me is Spanish Blue indeed.

The Enchantment

Often times, a working title is given to a piece that has just been written. As I sat and composed this waltz at the piano, I noticed out the window a young couple stroll by our home with their young child. They had just moved across the street into an old blue house and I seized that image, immediately naming this "The Blue House Waltz." After recording and then in frequent listening, I found myself drifting into a slightly altered state as this song played. This is now one of my all-time favorites, and I hope you feel this same sense of enchantment as you listen.

Her Solitude

Upon hearing this song shortly after I composed it, my mother, who was visiting with us for the day, knowing that I had not yet named it, remarked that "solitude" would be a fitting title. I took my mother's comment to heart and this song, and its title, is now dedicated to her.

First Snow

This piece (which I must thank my brother Gary for naming) seems the perfect title, for it does bring to mind the peaceful feeling one gets as pure white snow gently drifts from the sky and blankets the world for the first time in the winter season.

Turn Turn Turn (to everything there is a season)

I often come up with dozens of working titles for my CDs as well. One of these early titles was *A Time of Peace*, which is also a line from a hit song I first heard as a teenager performed by the band The Byrds back in 1965. Turn Turn Turn was composed and performed originally by the great folk artist, Pete Seeger, with the lyric being based on the King James version of the Bible. (Ecclesiastes 3, verses 1 - 8). The love I have of this song inspired me to do my own arrangement and the lyric still rings true to me today, especially the line, "A time for peace . . . I swear it's not too late."

Hymn

The simple movement and stately theme of this composition brought back memories of old-time hymns I had heard as a child. Hymns are defined as songs of praise and this piece, I feel, is most certainly spiritual in nature, but not specifically religious. The aspect of the divine and/or the object of the praise here are left up to each listener.

SANCTUARY ROSE (rondo in g minor)

evening song

As our life unfolds, we will eventually hear the song of our soul. It sings of our purpose and of the gifts we've been given to share. The soul is always singing . . . we need only listen.

midnight reverie

A willingness to explore and embrace our spiritual nature may open us to new insights, sudden flashes of enlightenment, and a heightened sense of clear inner vision. At times, these gifts and revelations are also seemingly thrust upon us, but always, they are there to guide and encourage us to look for the true meaning in life.

daybreak flower

Now the heart begins to open to its true divine nature. These insights and moments of enlightenment are moving us ever forward on the soul's journey home. In our heart of hearts . . . a flower blooms.

(rondo - a compositional form where the first and third musical sections are the same, with the second theme, being somewhat different.)

Sleeping Dove (Salish Lullaby)

I was given the honor of arranging the melody of this Salish lullaby into a solo piano piece first appearing on the CD *Heart Of The Bitterroot**telling the touching and powerful stories of four Salish and Pend d'Oreille Indian woman. Executive producer for this project, Julie Cajune, said that one of the last Salish men to play the flute, Jerome Vanderburg, first learned this lullaby from his father, who is said to have learned it from wild doves. Here, I dedicate this song to my friend Julie, to the generations of Salish and Pend d'Oreille woman who have come before, and to "women of good heart" everywhere.

*more information on *Heart Of The Bitterroot* available at http://www.npustin.org

PAINTING THE SUN

By DAVID LANZ

Moderately slow

p

With pedal

8

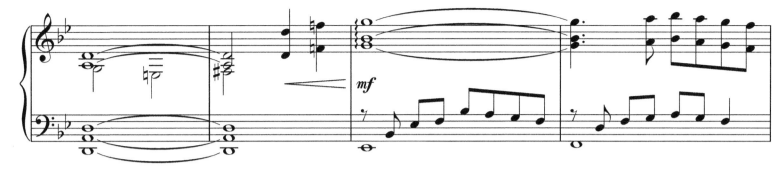

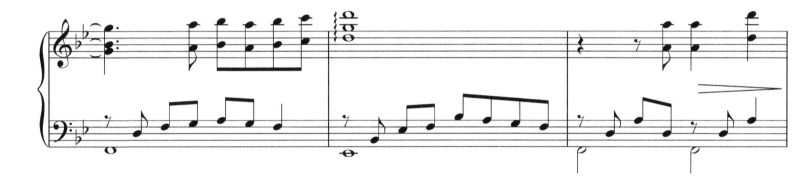

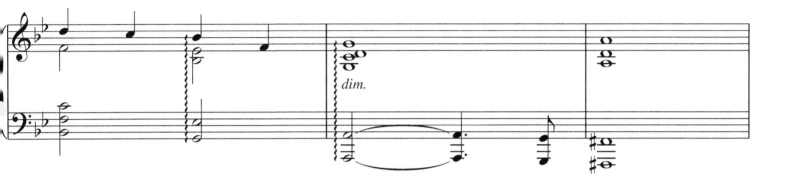

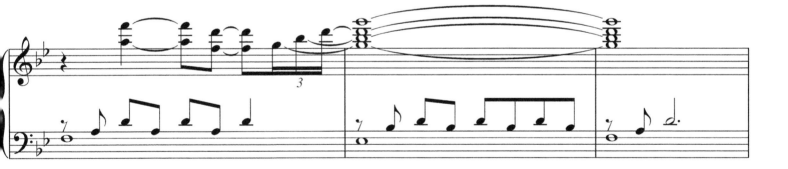

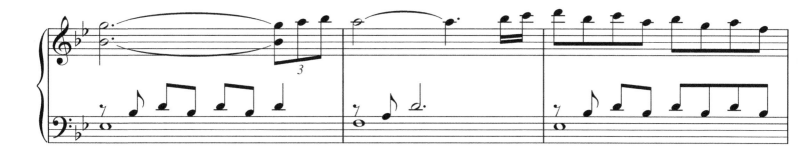

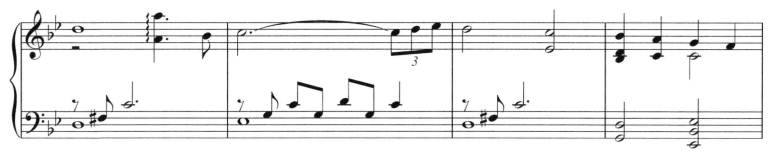

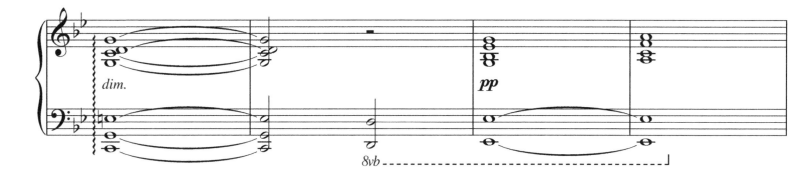

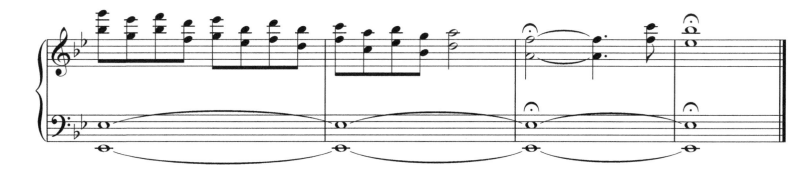

SPANISH BLUE

By DAVID LANZ

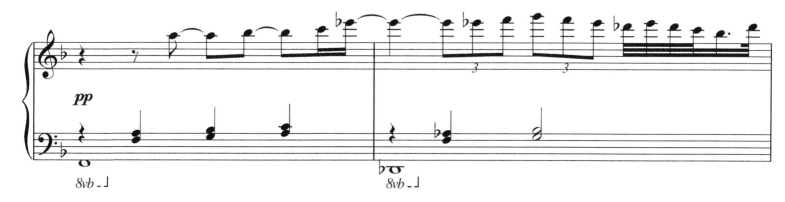

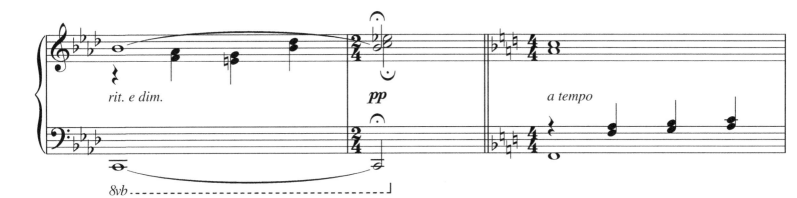

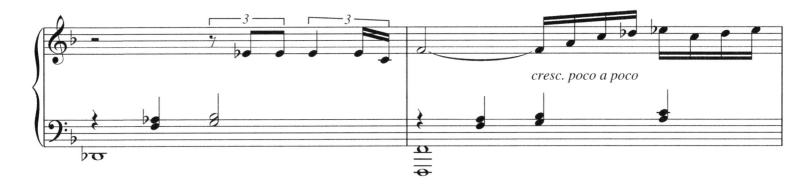

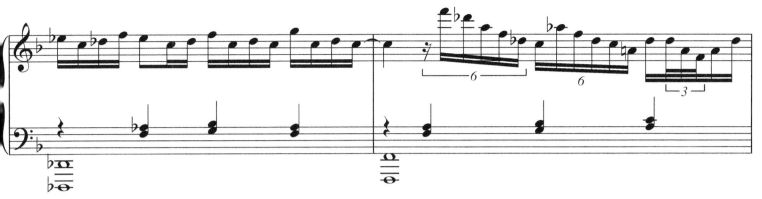

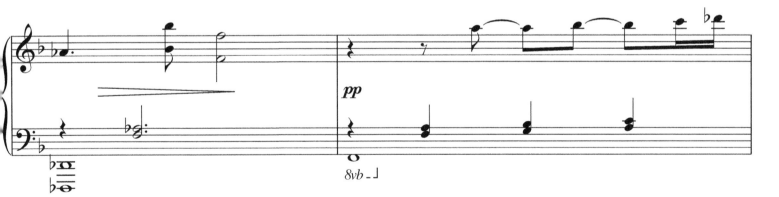

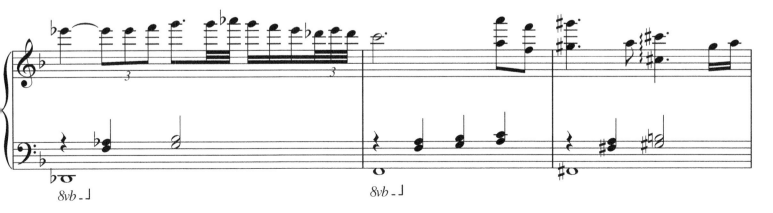

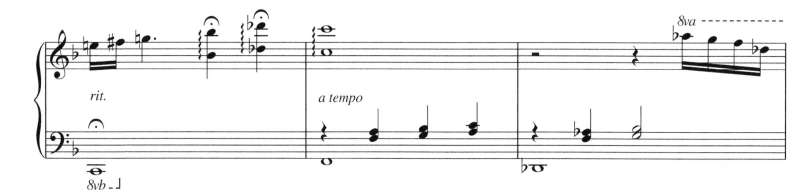

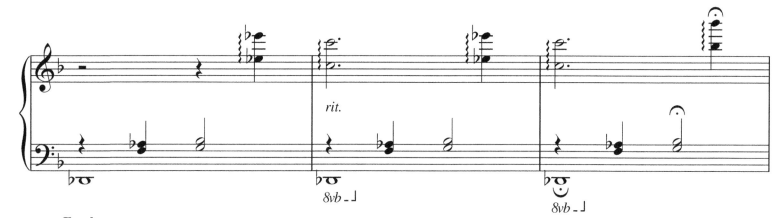

THE ENCHANTMENT

By DAVID LANZ

Waltz tempo

With pedal

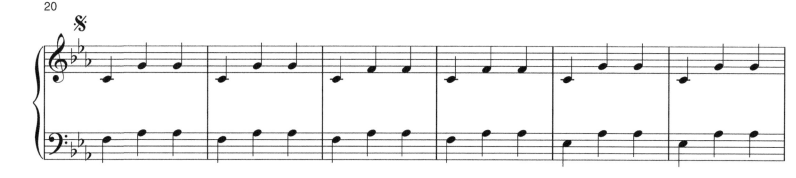

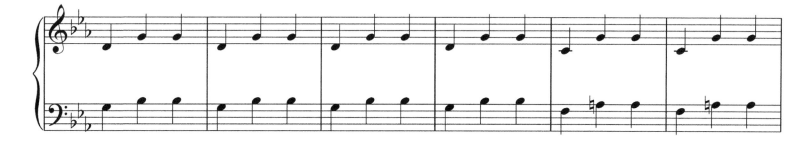

Play cues 2nd time:

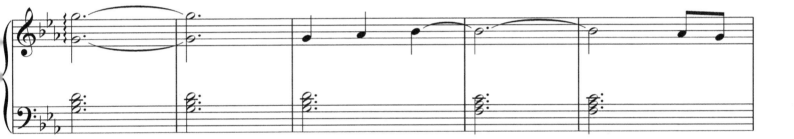

To Coda ⊕

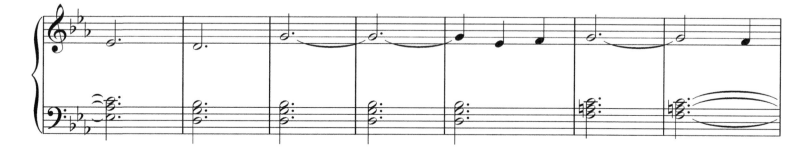

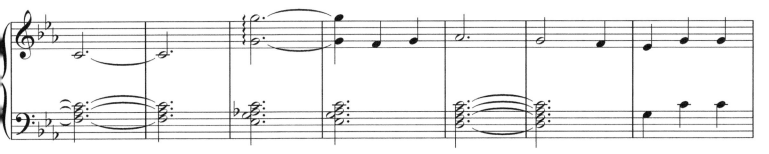

D.S. al Coda

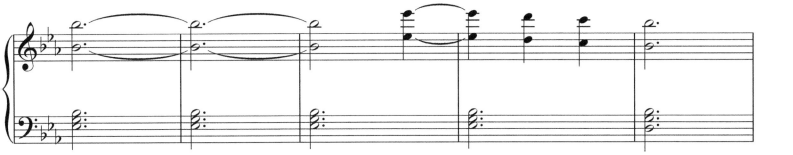

CODA

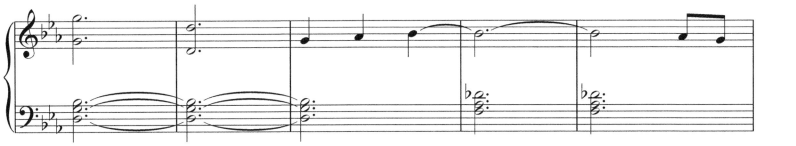

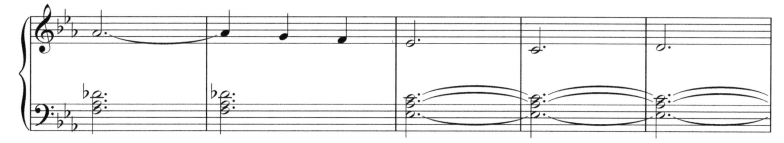

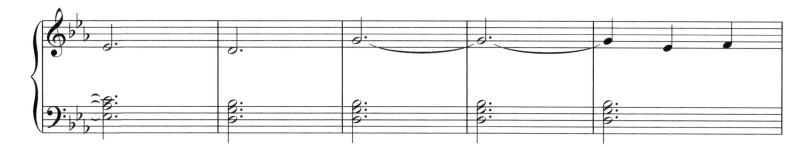

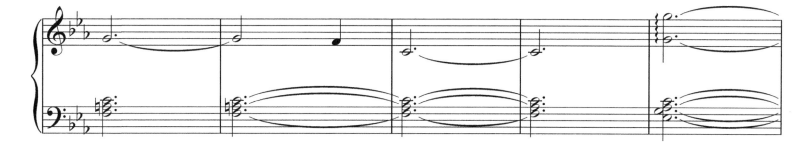

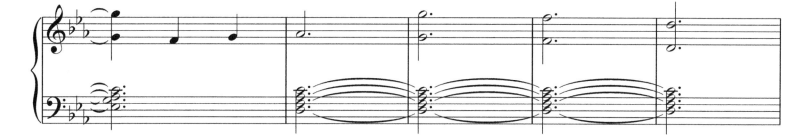

HER SOLITUDE

By DAVID LANZ

Slowly

With pedal

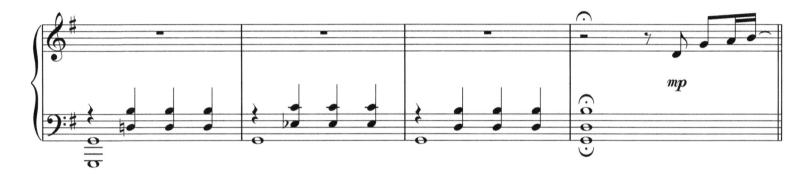

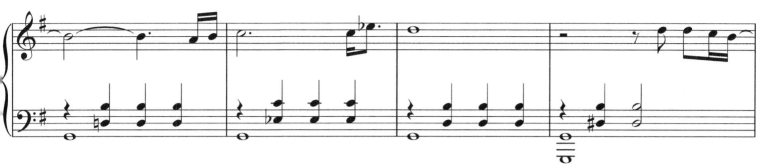

FIRST SNOW

By DAVID LANZ

Moderately

With pedal

To Coda ⊕

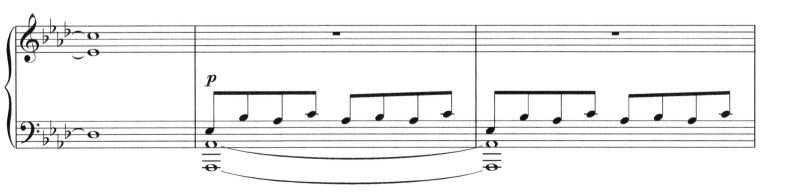

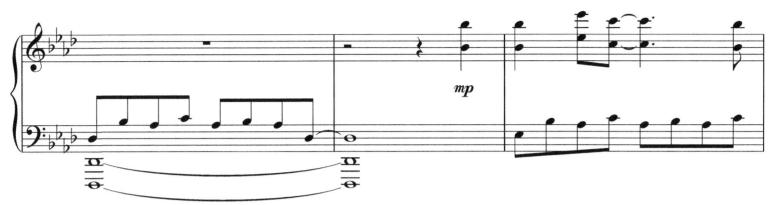

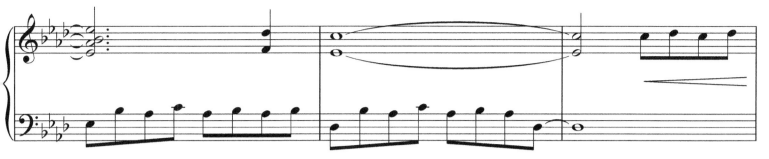

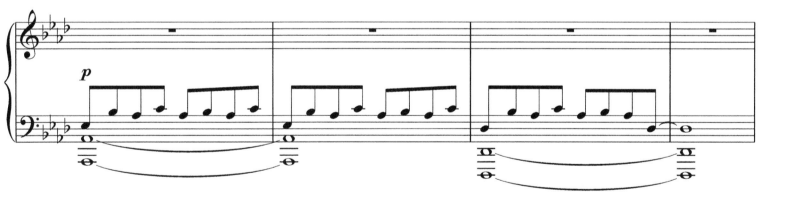

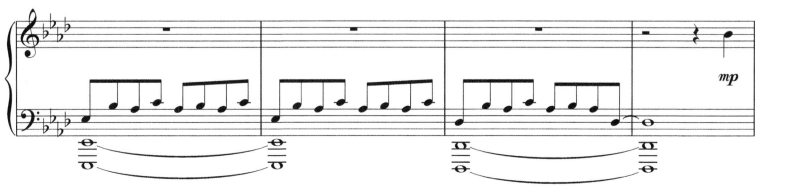

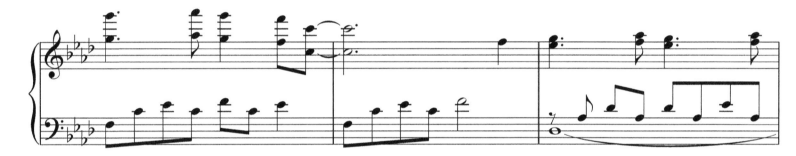

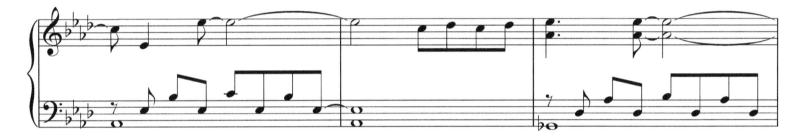

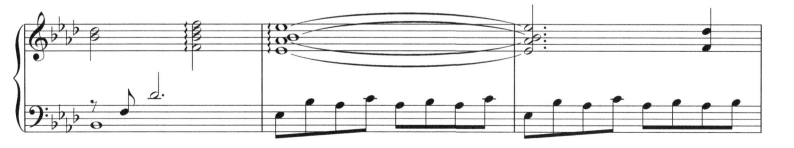

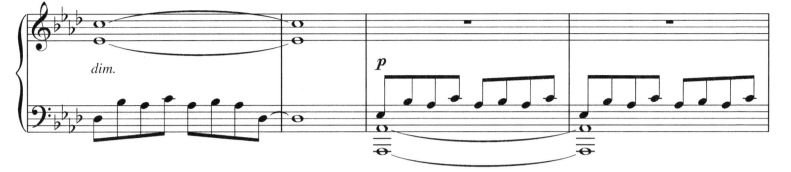

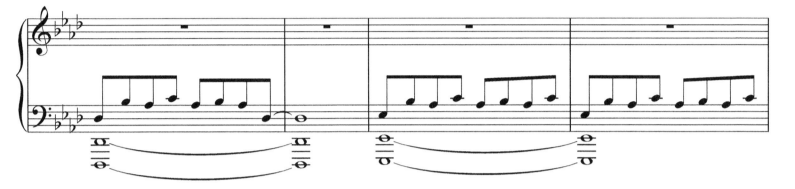

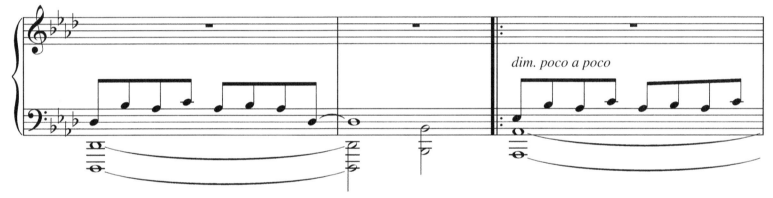

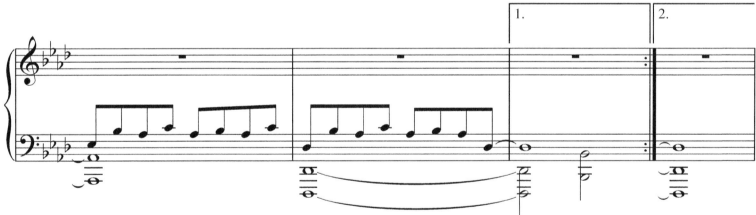

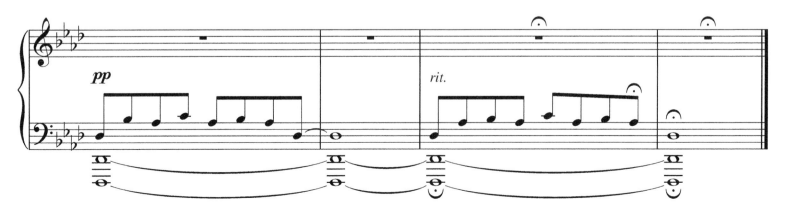

TURN! TURN! TURN!
(To Everything There Is a Season)

Words from the Book of Ecclesiastes
Adaptation and Music by
PETE SEEGER

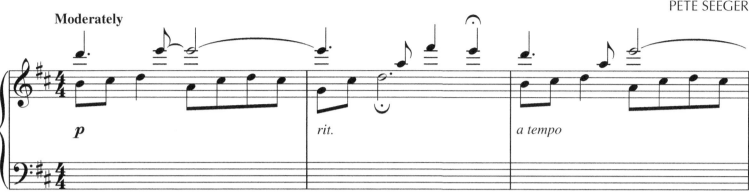

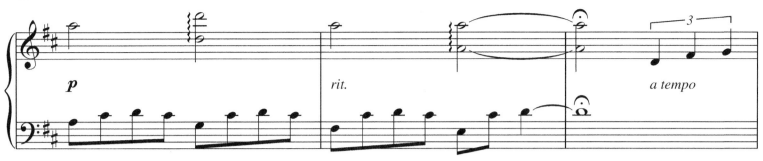

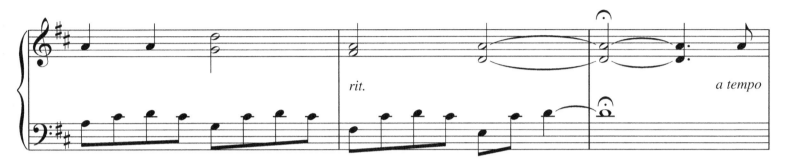

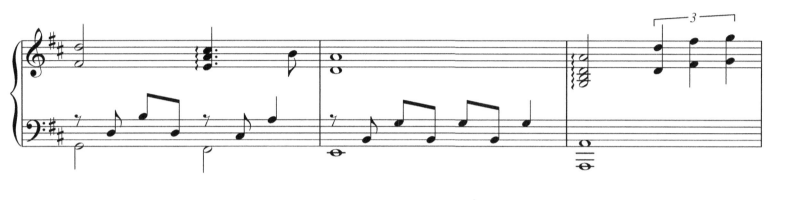

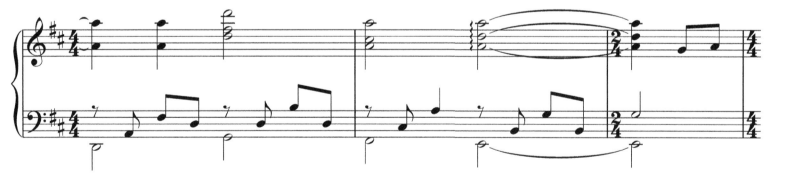

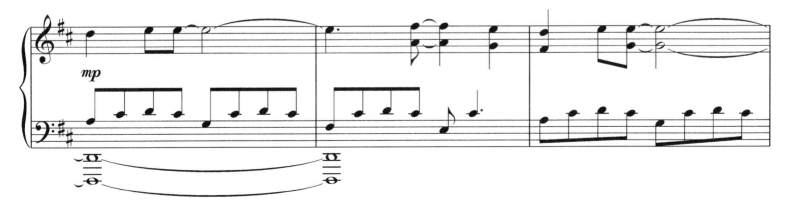

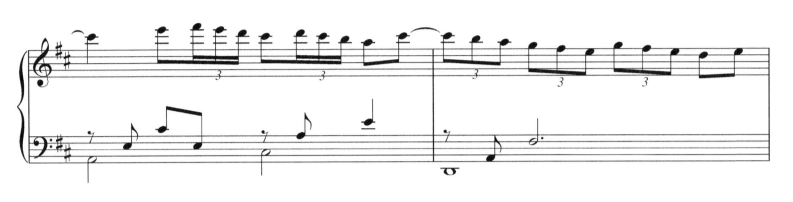

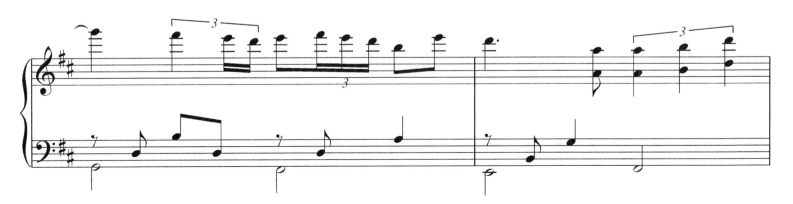

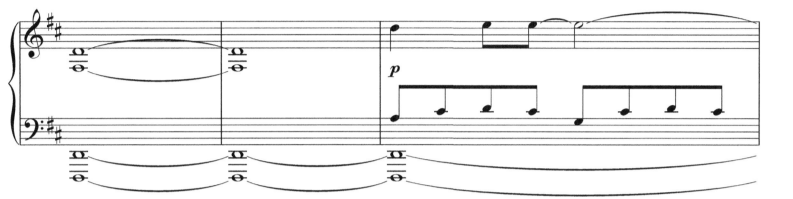

8va to end

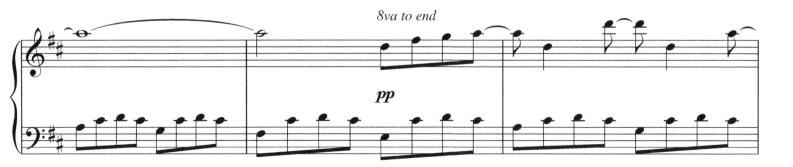

Repeat and Fade

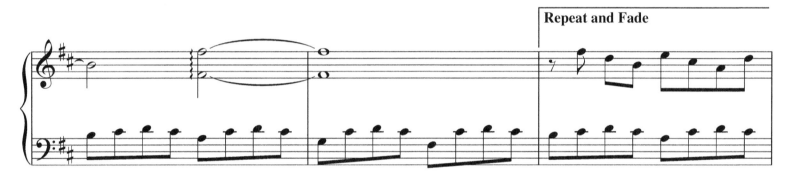

Optional Ending

rit.

HYMN

By DAVID LANZ

Moderately

mp

With pedal

SANCTUARY ROSE

(rondo in g minor)
1. evening song

By DAVID LANZ

Moderately slow

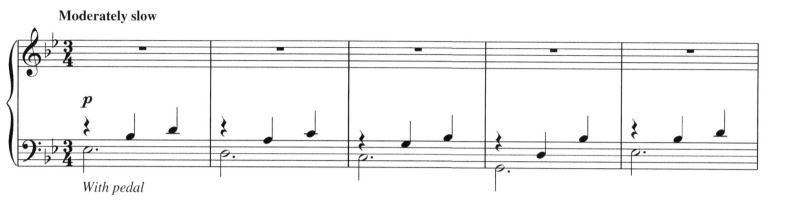

With pedal

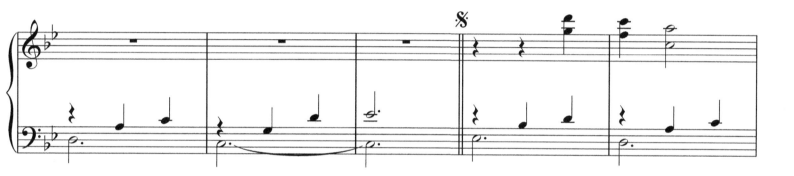

To Coda

54

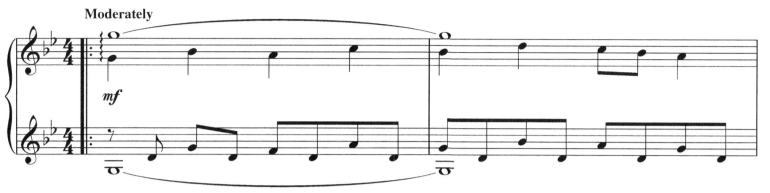

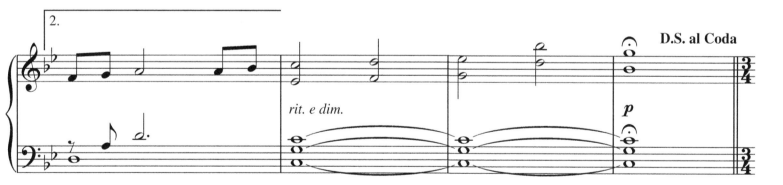

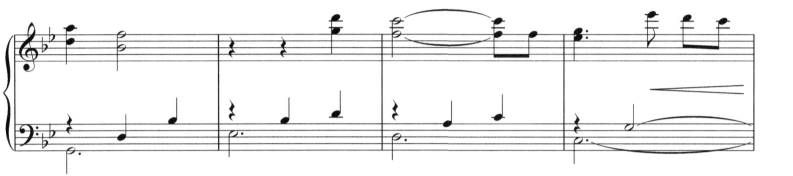

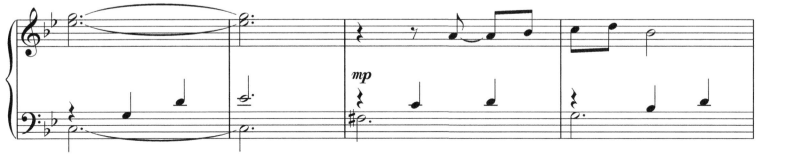

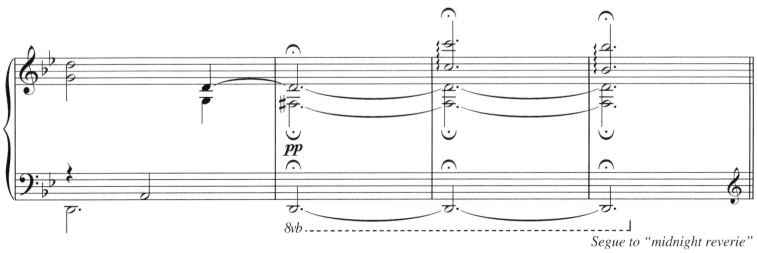

Segue to "midnight reverie"

2. midnight reverie

By DAVID LANZ

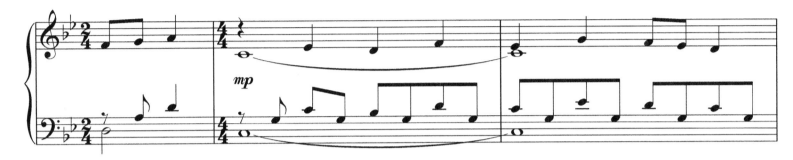

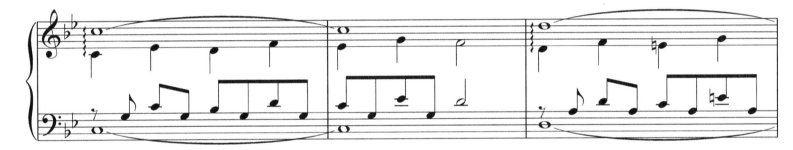

Segue to "daybreak flower"

3. daybreak flower

By DAVID LANZ

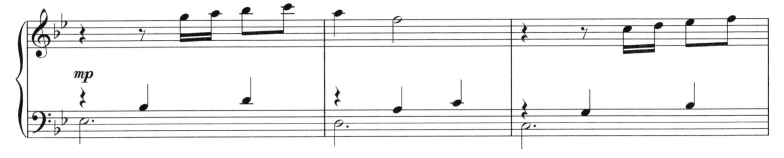

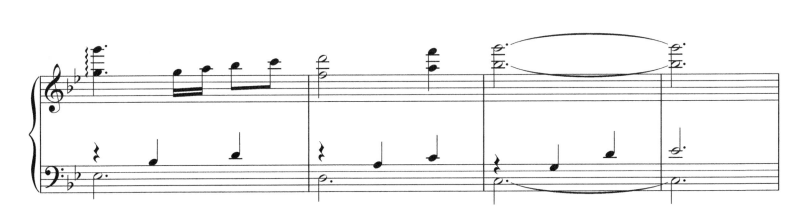

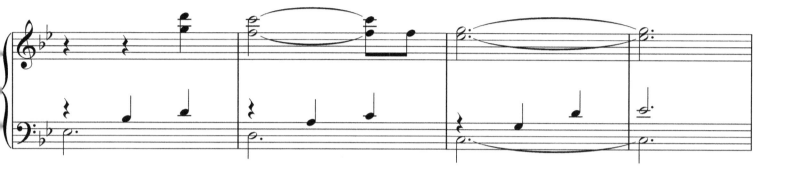

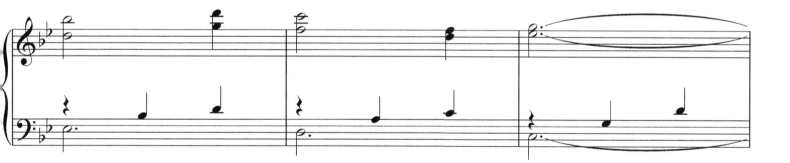

SLEEPING DOVE
(Salish Lullaby, from *Heart of the Bitterroot*)

By DAVID LANZ

Moderately fast, flowing

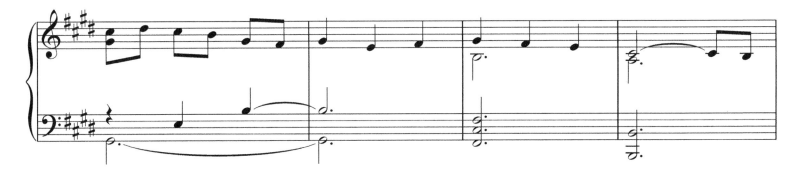

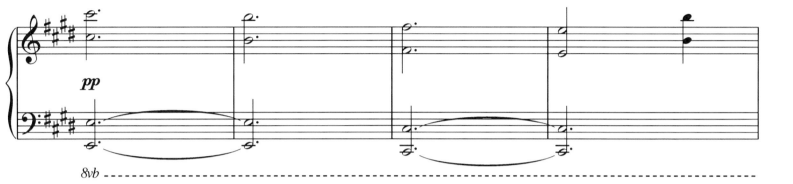

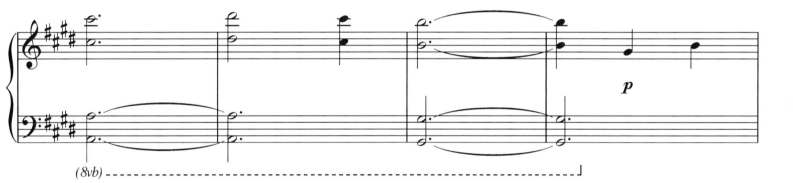

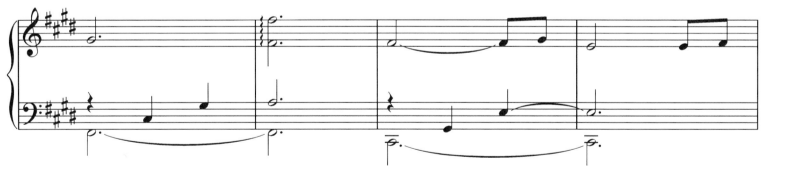

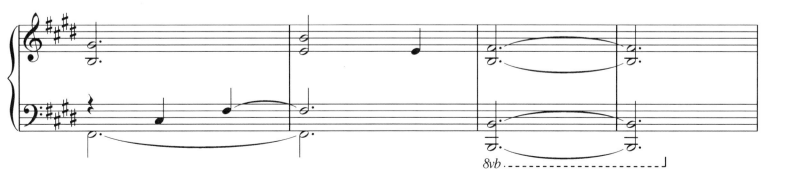

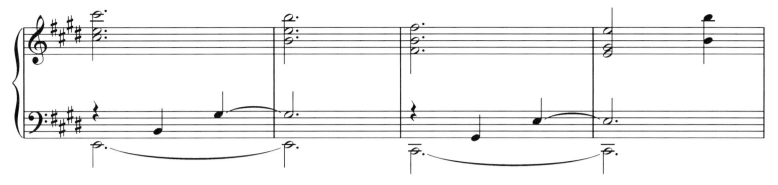

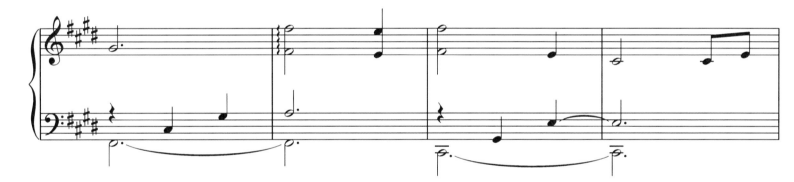

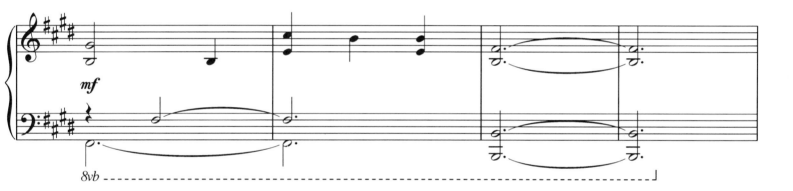

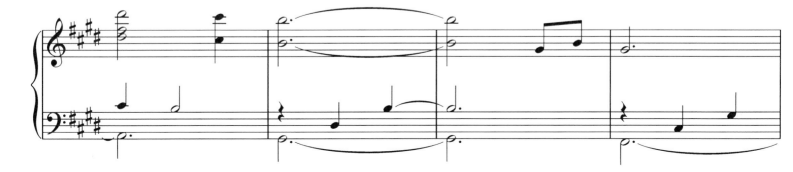

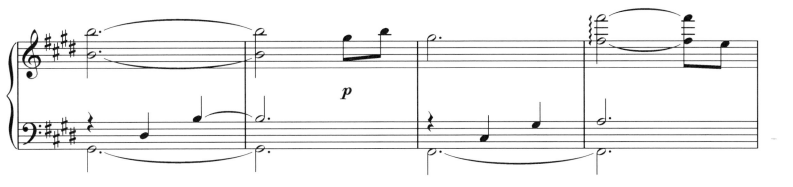

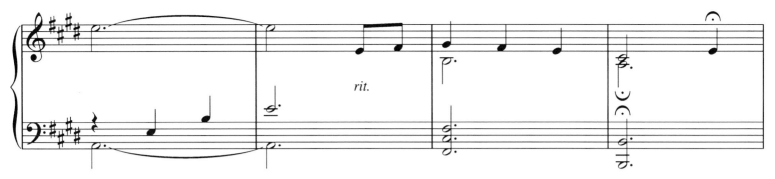

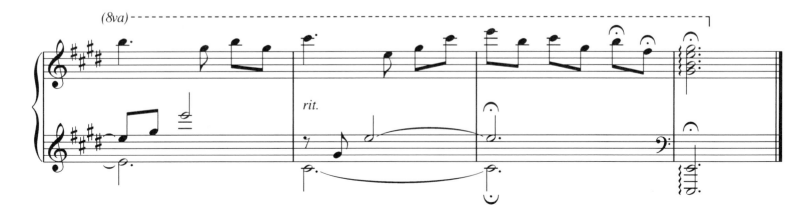